GERTIE

*Could there be angels among us,
ready and willing to assist, when
the time is right?*

Cynthia M. Long

First Printing, 2016
www.theredgown.com

This account is based on a true story. I have tried to recreate events, locales and conversations from memories of them. In order to maintain anonymity, in some instances, I have changed the names of individuals and some identifying characteristics and a few details.

To all the angel seekers and to the doubtful. May you encounter a miracle like Gertie before departing this earth.

Table of Contents

The Incredible Beginning

"Gertie, we need you!" I exclaimed.

Randy stared at me as we drove up and down the street to find a close restaurant parking spot. "Who's Gertie?" he asked.

"Gertie is one of my angels. One of her specialties is parking spots!"

"Are you kidding me?" Randy was now amused.

"Gertie, please, we need a close parking spot! Randy, please go back to the restaurant. We will find a perfect place to park the car."

Randy glanced over, puzzled.

"Okay. Let's try again!" Randy replied.

Randy and I drove right up to the restaurant. No parking spots. I inspected each side of the street. All of a sudden, someone pulled out right smack in front of the restaurant. Randy paused, acted surprised, and pulled in.

"Thank you, Gertie!" I was pleased to show Randy the magic.

Randy chuckled, "Thank you, Gertie!"

We got out of the car and entered the restaurant. We were seated right away.

Randy curiously asked, "Did you ask Gertie to help us get a seat right away?"

"No." I grinned and was floored he even thought of asking such a question.

We ordered a drink.

"Cin, tell me more about Gertie."

"Sure. It's a miraculous story," I responded.

1

I began reflecting upon the beginning of the Gertie story. It had been awhile since I repeated it to anyone and was trying to put it together in my mind before sharing it with Randy.

Randy was getting comfortable in his seat. He took a menu and placed it in front of himself and started scanning it, then he stopped and looked up.

"I know what I want."

I wasn't very hungry or interested in looking at the full menu.

"Me too. I just want the soup special."

Randy took my menu, placed it on top of his, with a welcoming grin to begin.

"Well…about fourteen years ago or so, I went to a spiritual class and was introduced to a meditative technique to connect to my guardian angel. There were about ten women gathered in a circle, ready to begin the process. We started by imagining that we were sitting in the middle row in an empty theater. We were told that there was a lever on the left side of one of the arms of the chair. This lever would open the plush red velvet theater curtain when we were ready to see our angel. Just as the curtain began to open, we needed to ask the angel their name.

"I sat there for only a few minutes with my eyes closed. While turning the lever, the velvet curtain was drawn. I opened my eyes and I asked my angel's name. There before me was an older woman with her hair pulled back in a bun, wearing an old-fashioned dress.

"'My name is Gertie,' she said. I closed my eyes tightly, pressed the lever on the arm-rest, and the curtain closed. I quickly reopened it and hoped to see a beautiful young angel with white feathered wings appear. But there stood the older woman with an inviting smile. Perplexed, I again asked her name. 'My name is Gertie.'

"I thought I didn't get the assignment. I closed the curtain disappointed and unsure. When everyone came out of contemplation, the sharing began.

"I listened to the other ladies talk of names like Angelica, Felicia, Miciella, etc., with flowing dresses, golden locks, and angel wings. It was then my turn to narrate the experience.

"'Gertie!' I uttered. 'My angel's name is Gertie, and she's an elder. She was wearing an old fashioned dress, and her hair was pulled back in a bun.'

"I knew I had made a mistake. I was remarkably disturbed. No one saw anything remotely close to what I had witnessed that winter eve many years ago. As I attentively watched the women in the circle, a few chuckled, some were very amused, and others weren't so sure I had gotten the assignment right either. The evening ended. I walked to my car shaking my head in disbelief. I was down on myself for a few days after that."

The Twilight Zone Meeting

The waitress returned with our drinks.

"Cin, what a name: Gertie? It's such an old-fashioned name," Randy added.

"Yes, it is. I was considerably unsure about the entire experience. Something started to happen in the weeks following, though. I began hearing the names, Gertie and Gertrude. What are the odds of this old-fashioned name appearing again in this ultra-modern world? I held on to the synchronicities and took notice that something was up with these signs.

"As the years unfolded, more came into light, and I became spiritually in tune. I began talking to Gertie, asking for assistance, especially for parking spaces and—oh my—she never failed to find a perfect parking spot! Just like this evening!"

Randy smiled.

"Others in my life started using Gertie, but I informed them that they had their own angels and was important to access them. I didn't want her to get worn out! Gertie is still highly revered, especially by my young adult children."

Randy and I were both chuckling then.

"About eight years ago, I took a death and dying class. It was formally known as Compassion in Action, and now The Twilight Brigade. I wanted it to become part of my life's work to assist people in transition. Dannion Brinkley, who had at least three near-death experiences, developed this heartfelt training weekend.

4

It truly changed my life!"

"Dannion Brinkley? I never heard of him." Randy was eager to know more about the man.

"Dannion was in special forces in Vietnam, and part of his healing and work was to be of service to those dying. I don't know much about the Vietnam part, but the little I've learned was startling. In regards to his near-death experience, I believe the story goes like this. One day he was sitting on his couch in his living room talking on the phone, and a bolt of lightning reached straight into the phone line, struck and killed him. He was dead for twenty-eight minutes and was then revived, which was a miracle in itself."

"What? How can someone be dead for twenty-eight minutes?" Randy was puzzled.

"I've come to trust there are many things we don't know unless we're up close to a similar situation. But there are thousands upon thousands of individuals who have had near-death experiences and are beginning to speak out, like Dannion. And me too."

"You too?"

"Yes. Another story for another time, Randy."

Randy lifted his brow with curiosity.

"Dannion then went to the other side, or heaven as most call it, and was told interesting things about the events in the world and his life. Altogether now, he's had like three near-death experiences. He was even shown things that turned out to be true years later. Dannion returned to not only tell his story, but it also changed him so profoundly that he dedicated his life to helping people transition. Specifically, our veterans, since many die alone."

"Wow, sounds like a profound man."

"Indeed."

The waitress emerged. Randy ordered our meals and refocused on me.

"Cin, this is better than any movie out there right now!"

"You haven't heard anything yet." I grinned.

"In the months that passed after I took that wondrous death and dying class, I received a call from a Compassion in Action friend. He asked if it was possible for me to take over an assignment, helping an elder transition, because he had an emergency to attend. Back then, I was working two businesses and was worn out. I felt this unbelievable tingle up and down my spine. The nudges wouldn't let up. Nudges were a significant indicator when it was vital I pay attention or move forward on a pending situation. I was certain I needed to take the assignment.

"I was asked by Steven to call the coordinator, Nadia, and she would fill me in on the details. She was in charge of the northern California area for that organization. Nadia explained the details of my first assignment, including the fact that the elder was dying of stomach cancer. When she mentioned the elder's name, I was taken aback! Gertrude."

"Hmmm…"

"I asked if Gertrude's nickname was Gertie. Nadia didn't know. After I received all the information necessary, we ended our conversation, and I was extremely anxious to meet this Gertrude."

"Gertrude? What are the odds of that name showing up in your life again?" Randy interjected.

"Wild, isn't it? Just wait, there's so much more."

Randy paid close attention. He took a sip of his

drink and was eager for me to continue.

"A few evenings passed, and I walked to Gertrude's hospital room in anticipation. As I entered the room, there before me was the woman who showed up in my vision during the Guardian Angel meditation class, many years ago—but how in the world could this be? Angels were supposed to be in spirit."

"Cynthia, are you serious? This isn't for real." Randy laughed.

"For real, Randy. For real." I smiled as I continued.

Wisdom From An Old Soul

"Gertie's hair was pulled back; her face was exactly how I remembered it when I was in the meditation class. I was absolutely stunned and all but paralyzed by this almost-paranormal meeting. I took a seat. As I sat there in complete and utter silence, it felt surreal watching Gertrude and her daughter converse. I thought I was in one of those parallel universes people talk about.

"While they were busy with each other, I reviewed the meditation class experience in my mind, combing over every detail. I also took notice of the photos that surrounded Gertrude's small space: Mother Teresa, the Dalai Lama, also another Indian-looking guru. And then, a photo of Gertrude and her daughter. Gertrude was wearing the same style of dress I saw in my vision. I took a deep breath and just sat there, numb."

"The same dress that was in your vision? Now you're scaring me," Randy said.

"I don't remember the color, but I remember the style. Tell me about it!" I added. "The photos of the guru and Mother Teresa gave a sense of comfort that I could probably tell my story to her! I held on to this unimaginable secret for about four days. I then felt confident enough to share it with Gertrude the next evening.

"'Has anyone ever called you Gertie?' Gertrude's face lit up through the suffering, like a bright and shining star.

"Only one other person called me by that name many years ago, dear. A special man who was the love of my life!" she replied.

"I took a cautious breath and proceeded to reveal my Gertie story with her. I fixedly gazed at her as I poured out my heart. She smiled steadily and nodded her head through the details and quietly waited. It was as if she had a special message.

"'Please call me Gertie, dear. I am your angel. It was time for us to meet!'"

Randy was now shaking his head in disbelief.

"My excitement amplified, Randy! I thought angels were not in a body. How was it possible?" I repeated, "How was it conceivable?"

Randy was now on the edge of his seat waiting for more.

"I sat there wanting to ask her question after question, but I couldn't speak. My mind was running in numerous directions. I guess it was crucial to just be and take in this confusing experience. Gertie and I ended our evening. As I was driving home, I continued to hear in my mind, I am your angel, it was time to meet. I kept saying it over and over. How was it possible? I narrated it to a few friends the next day and they were as perplexed as I was."

"I've never heard of such a thing. But, believe it or not, I've not been aware of many of the things you've already shared since we re-met! Cynthia Long, you are one fascinating person!"

"I don't know about fascinating. It's more like mainstream unusual!" I replied in a joking manner.

"Steven returned and we spent about a week more with Gertie before she passed on. We touched upon a myriad of feelings, memories of personal history, and the wisdom from her soul. I got to ask several questions, and she was very generous to answer, even when the pain of her cancer took over. I would ask Gertie to stop at times, witnessing her agony, but she insisted and continued on.

"One of the burning questions I asked Gertie was if she had anything significant to share that changed the course of her life for the better. Gertie thought about it and said, 'yes, it's about forgiveness. We must come to a place to forgive everyone who has ever hurt us. Forgive ourselves for those we have hurt. And make an effort to heal the issues within and without.'

Randy was paying rapt attention to my story. He asked a most curious question that I also wondered about.

"What does without mean? It sounds contradictory."

"Yes, I also had to stop and explore this term as it was unfamiliar. I never asked Gertie but because she was into the Eastern mystical traditions, it sounded like it came from one of the guru's teachings. My understanding, it's about healing what's outside of us. In this case, the person we're having a conflict with."

Gertrude continued her story, stating at different points in her life that she thought forgiveness was not achievable. "I was so invested in my own torment that forgiveness could never break through my stubbornness. But then, I had an epiphany after I had a conversation with someone very important. "Forgiveness isn't about the other person, initially. It's about you and your healing. But if you want to reach higher on the forgiveness ladder, it can bring the level of forgiving someone up a notch to a greater degree of consciousness, if one can forgive on this level. Unfortunately, some won't ever reach the beginning stages of forgiveness.

"Gertie, I don't completely understand," I replied to her.

Gertie pondered. She reached up and took a long strand of hair from the tightly placed bun on her head and began twirling it. It was as if this quirk helped her in some way. After a few seconds of twirling, Gertie continued.

"Let's take the example of someone I knew who lost her beautiful twenty-year-old daughter. She was kidnapped and killed by a man who was crazed on drugs. Joan, this young girl's mother, after too many difficult years of excruciating torment, searched high and low to get over that tragedy. She wanted closure but couldn't get there. Joan finally arrived at a place where she wanted to completely forgive this man for killing her beautiful child. After much contemplation, Joan wrote him a letter while he was in prison. She thought this would be the solution. And even when the man wrote back, it still didn't get her to a degree of peace Joan yearned for. She knew there was still more spiritual work to do. Joan then knew it was integral to meet him, eye-to-eye, heart-to-heart.

"How difficult it must have been, but Joan had the courage to at least attempt to heal from such a tragedy. When the face-to-face meeting took place, intense tears were shed, and so many pent up feelings that were harming both of them were loosened and released. Tremendous healing was now possible. Joan finally let go of all her hurt and resentment. This day she was able to truly listen to this man's story—Joan was only invested in her own up to that point. It was necessary to hear its entirety to come to a compassionate place. The man also released the agonizing misery of taking a vibrant young woman's life—something that probably would have never happened if he hadn't been addicted to drugs."

"Yes, he made a tragic choice, for sure. I see what you mean now. There are many missing parts to lots of stories, I believe. How many people have only a part of the story, and how many are still in pain because of it?" I replied.

"Most people never look past their own pain or story. Stories can create judgment of others, especially one-sided stories, yet it's the story that provides the opportunity and can activate the forgiveness process. A story helps some to get there...or not. A choice one makes. The ultimate goal, though, for the two parties involved in the story is to learn, grow, and heal. On the highest level, a story isn't necessary."

I was deep in thought about this statement. I had never heard of this before. "Gertie, what do you mean, on the highest level, a story isn't necessary?" I asked, perplexed.

"Those who have reached this degree of understanding—they don't want or need to hear the story. They already know; people are where they're supposed to be. They understand that we are not just our body, our personality traits, and the choices we make. We are souls who have come here to evolve. Those who have chosen tough lessons will evolve faster, no doubt, if they learn, grow, and ultimately take the information and apply it in a useful manner."

"Very interesting..."

"Eventually, Joan began working in the prison system teaching inmates how to forgive. Out of tragedy, came a blessing. But this mother was willing and ready to reach another level of forgiveness. This was so extreme; few can reach it at this point."

I was breathless. I didn't know what to say to Gertie, as I had never heard anyone who forgave in that manner. To forgive someone who has murdered their child? That was unbelievable!

I reflected again. "Gertie, isn't this what Christ's ministry was about?"

True Love Is Very Real

"Christ was a master teacher of the true meaning of unconditional love. Forgiveness is the ultimate pathway to true love."

"Yes." I nodded. "Gertie, I'm curious, who did you have this conversation with that helped you?"

"Christi, my daughter. Christi helped me in this process." Gertie floated off into the distance, her eyes tearing up.

* * *

"Cin, that is mind blowing!" Randy paused and contemplated.

"I'm now re-examining my own forgiveness issues," he said.

"Yes, most of us have them lurking around."

"There was one last thing Gertie was determined to make known. Have you had enough?"

"Cin, please go on. This is almost like a lifetime of therapy."

* * *

One evening when I arrived, Gertie was all propped up in her hospital bed, her hair neatly pulled back in her favorite bun style. It felt as though she was excitedly prepared to open up. I couldn't read her mannerisms exactly, but it appeared Gertie wanted to get started right away.

"Dear, there's something critically important I

want you to begin to understand."

I took a seat, placed my hand bag down on the side of the worn, stuffed chair, and squirmed around to get in a comfortable position.

"What is it, Gertie?"

"Have you ever been in love? A love beyond anything you ever could imagine?" she asked. I didn't understand her point, or where Gertie was going with that question.

"Well, I was married for twenty years and thought I was in love. But it didn't feel like true love after a while—couldn't have been. I don't believe true love ends," I replied to her.

"No, true love doesn't end, Cin." Gertie was then smiling affectionately. The dim twinkle in her tired, yet determined eyes was affecting me in a mystical way— almost as if Gertie wanted me to open up like never before. Soul-to-soul.

"Let me ask you in this manner. Go back to the events where you felt you were deeply in love. It's sometimes called the honeymoon stage." Gertie was hopeful I would absorb the lesson quickly by giving an example.

"Yes, I've had a few honeymoon-stage relationships. Looking back, my two-year courtship with my husband was a honeymoon stage. The twenty-year marriage had more of those moments when the children were small. After the divorce, I had a four-year relationship with a man, but we took a break from one another, and he supposedly found a new love. After a while, he wanted to come back, which I pondered, but then felt it wouldn't work." I slowly and thoughtfully replied in retrospect as I tried to recall.

"And when this stage ended, or better yet, that person left your life, how did you feel?" Gertie asked.

"I can say it was challenging. No one ever wants the romantic feeling to end. This kind of love is what everyone desires. Look at the romance industry; it's a billion-dollar empire because it all boils down to the entire world desiring love," I replied.

I stopped briefly to recall more wondrous past moments. "I remember when my sweet, late aunt materialized in a corner of the hospital room where one of my elderly uncles had spent his last days. My late aunt was waiting for him to pass away so that she could take him home. When I told my aunt that I missed her, she opened her arms and enveloped every part of my body. It was like the love of heaven entered my entire being. It was that astounding. I actually almost fell off my chair while in tears. The love she sent was that powerful. I didn't want that feeling to end, Gertie."

"The birth and childhood stages of my children, who loved unconditionally and thought I was the greatest human on the planet, were fleeting but also profound. I also had elevated feelings of love when I went to heaven during my NDE. The NDE, though, felt similar to the honeymoon period of a relationship." I paused, my NDE thoughts popped out of my head and into the clouds of heaven. My body reacted intimately, breaking out in goose bumps. It was all a glorious remembering. Seconds later, new thoughts jumped back in my head, and I continued.

Gertie was observing my mannerisms.

"Oh, I forgot, there were a few times I had spiritual occurrences, and it was a heightened feeling as well."

"But for now, let's just talk about the breakup of a relationship between two people. One withdrawing from the other."

"Okay," I hesitantly replied. I still wasn't sure where Gertie was going with this.

"When the other person withdrew his love, how did you feel?" she asked.

"Horrible. It was like my heart dropped into the pit of my stomach. I ached and couldn't function." Then I recalled a few such relationship episodes.

"And when we withdraw our love from another it's a different experience altogether, isn't it?" Gertie asked.

"Yes, of course." I readjusted my posture since I felt a little uneasy reminiscing about a few past connections I had left unfinished. "Reflecting back, one was a teenage relationship and another, my husband. He never wanted to sit down and talk about any issues during the marriage. It always ended in an argument, with him storming out of the house. He didn't want to learn or work towards a better relationship. After many years of struggle, I gave up."

Gertie courteously listened, then added, "True love between two people isn't just about the couple actually. It's about each person individually learning the intricacies to find true love within. This is an example of each soul indirectly assisting the other to get to this magical place, through the romance stage of a relationship. The key is to stay in this blessed place, if the other is present or if he or she has left the relationship, physically or emotionally. Humanity doesn't truly understand romance yet."

"I guess I don't understand romance either.

Wow, Gertie, this would be a new concept for most."

"Romance is a trigger for what each person is capable of achieving within. Romance mostly ends because we feel it's the other party who is responsible for the demise of the relationship. That person has withdrawn their love, and they are supposedly making the other person experience a terrible heartbreak. So, when perceived love is withheld, or ends, it feels as if we're disconnected, and to reconnect, we assume we need another person, which is a facade.

"Have you ever met someone and immediately felt the sparks of attraction ignited? You knew somehow that this person was meant to be in your life and you instinctively wanted to be close, and you might have even thought that you could spend the rest of your life with that person?" Gertie's eyes were wide with excitement and all wound up. She obviously felt very strongly about this subject for some reason. It sounded like she experienced this attraction with the love of her life.

"I've felt glimpses of this, Gertie. I would love to be in the midst of such a feeling always. I'm fascinated by those who are still in love after many years. I know dozens of couples. I can only recollect one who is in love like that."

"That instinctive connection is clearly about one soul recognizing another from a different time and place. More often than not, the connection is so uncanny that it almost feels impossible, but it is all part of God's plan."

"Yes, Gertie. I'm reminded of a story of a woman whose husband left her for another. She was so miserable and couldn't function for months. One early morning, she decided to get in her car and just drive. She ended up at a roadside diner, a hundred miles from her home at three in the morning. She entered the diner and took a seat. There was a man who sat two stools over from her. The man noticed that she was in a sad state and attempted to cheer her up. He began to engage her in a conversation. They ended up talking for hours. One thing led to another, and a year later she married him. She felt it was destiny that brought them together. They have been married for over thirty years now. If she hadn't gotten into her car that early morning hour and driven to that diner, would it have been a lost opportunity?"

"If it was meant to be, it could never be lost," Gertie responded.

"My cousin also had a heartbreaking experience. She was married to her first husband when she was only sixteen. He left her for another woman, when my cousin was in her forties. She was distressed for years. I felt and mentioned that there was someone else for her. I could just sense it, perhaps the love of her life. She was ambivalent, but a few years later, this special man walked into her life out of the blue. In retrospect, she saw it differently."

"Again, God always has a plan. Her time with her first husband was up, but given that she had no faith and trust in the greater plan, she suffered immensely, I imagine. Obviously, she didn't understand that true love isn't just about the other person. Her first husband's soul gave her the opportunity to learn this important lesson," Gertie responded.

"I still don't believe she gets the opportunity and true love part."

"For another time, my dear. If one goes out in the world and asks randomly about stories like the ones

19

you've just narrated, there would be an endless supply of similar connections. Often times, those coupling for shorter durations need to have the experience of having children specifically for the lessons they will all learn along the way."

"I believe this too, Gertie."

"If humanity understood romance, practiced and lived this life lesson, there would be fewer breakups; more people would be in the state of "true love" and self-satisfied with a partner or without. It all begins within."

Gertie took a piece from her bun and began twirling it while in contemplation. Her kind, fatigued eyes held my attention.

"Sweet child, this is your life journey and yours alone. Every situation and person added into your life is for your growth. We are humans having a spiritual experience. We emerged from love, and love should be our natural state of being. Children inherently know this."

"Gertie, so what you are saying is that I should live as if I'm in romantic love even when I'm alone?" I still wasn't grasping the lesson she was trying to teach.

"Alone or not! The fact is, love can never be taken away. We give too much power to others and discount our own true nature. Cin, you must become quiet and learn to get to know your soul better. This, in turn, will help you to live with greater love in your life."

Gertie's tone was slowing down at that point. I knew it was necessary to end our conversation on this subject matter.

"I'm going to put this on the back burner for now; it's pretty advanced."

Gertie took a breath and responded firmly and

convincingly. "Dear, take it in small doses. Once you get this understanding and live it, your life will change dramatically."

She paused and drifted off, holding her strand of hair. She refocused and carefully watched as I stood and prepared to leave.

"Cin, you must learn to meditate. It will be life changing."

"I took a class a few years back, but I still haven't incorporated meditation into my life."

I walked over, hugged her, and said my goodbyes. Our embrace was noticeably longer that evening. I felt we might be close to the end of our time together, which was distressing to imagine.

After Death Connection

"Randy, it was very clear. I wasn't just there to help Gertie's transition. I was mainly there for her to reveal the insight I was destined to hear before she passed on. I was saddened that our connection was brief, but it was meant to be—in the human form, anyway. Her body was quickly fading, and her spirit was ready to soar."

"Yes, you were there for a bigger reason, for sure… I'm not getting the romance part. It's too far out there for me." Randy was noticeably uncomfortable.

"Likewise myself." I smiled with affection.

"Did you ever ask Gertie if she lived this sort of romantic state in her own life?"

"No, I just assumed she was far advanced into this stage. I was so taken by the concept and somewhat hypnotized, my mind was stuck and focused on my past relationships, which were all great examples of romantic disconnect."

I sat there in a melancholy state, reviewing my last statement. I was still in the same place emotionally as when Gertie and I had that last conversation on romantic love. Little had changed in that direction, except that I took her advice and began meditating.

"Cin, are you okay?" asked Randy when he noticed my dispirited mood.

"I'm fine. For years I placed this entire lesson aside and am just reviewing it now. It reminded me of some aching circumstances."

I took a deep breath. "Gertie passed away not too

long after Steven returned. I attended her small funeral service. I went on with my life. But then…"

The waitress returned with our meal. She placed our plates in front of us and we picked up our utensils.

"Cin, please continue."

"Randy, let's talk about this another time."

We finished our meal in silence.

"Cin, you're awfully quiet. Did I say something to offend you?"

"Not at all. I get this way every so often."

We left the restaurant and Randy drove straight for my car. We got out. Randy asked for my keys, opened the driver's door, ushered me inside, and gave a heartfelt hug.

"Thank you for the pleasant evening. I'll call you tomorrow."

"Okay. Thank you for listening. Hope it wasn't too uncomfortable?"

"Not at all. Cannot wait to hear the rest."

* * *

On the way home from Randy's, I recalled the synchronicities between Christi and I, months after Gertie's passing. One day while I was driving to Los Altos, I remembered that it was important to stop at the bank—a task I'd put off that week. Impatiently standing in line, I noticed Gertie's daughter, Christi. I got her attention but she didn't make a connection at first. We conversed for a few minutes and both went on our separate ways. I didn't feel it was unusual, and I went on with my life.

A year or more later, I placed an ad in the

newspaper for my services as a personal assistant because I needed more clients—the Bay Area was populated by well over a million people. One day, I picked up my phone messages to see if I had any potential clients. One person's voice stood out, and I was extremely curious if that was Gertie's daughter. I called the woman back and discovered it was Christi. At first, it was challenging to understand that coincidence since she didn't know anything about me or my business. We were both amazed. We chatted away about insignificant topics until I got a nudge to unearth the following.

"Christi, there was a conversation I had with your mother before she passed. I forgot to mention it to you. Every so often I thought to myself, why didn't I mention this to Christi? I know you would want to hear it. In my opinion, your mother has had a hand in connecting us once again. I asked your mother if there was anything that changed the course of her life and if she would be so kind to share."

Christi was silent and eager to hear.

"Gertie said we must forgive ourselves for those we have hurt. Forgive everyone who has ever hurt us, and make an effort to heal the situation."

"I assisted my mother in this process?" Christi began to tear up.

"Yes, it seems so."

"Now that I look back, my mother would become very still when I would mention forgiveness in any form or fashion. It now makes sense. She was obviously observing and perhaps taking the information to apply it to her own forgiveness issues."

I gave Christi space to digest and collect herself.

Christi mentioned that she was still trying to cope

with her mother's death. I made some effort to comfort her after the news given. We ended our conversation, and life went on until the next synchronicity with Christi.

It occurred during a church seminar from the previous year. I had been sitting among fifty or so people scattered here and there throughout the church. A speaker had just finished up, and we had a short break. I began talking with a man sitting close by, and the topic of angels surfaced. I felt a need to tell him about my Gertie story. As I was reminiscing, minutes later I sensed that someone sat right behind my chair while I was sharing the uncanny synchronicities of the encounter. I turned around after I was finished, and who was in back of me? Gertie's daughter, Christi! We jumped up, hugged each other, almost screaming in excitement, but didn't want to disturb the other participants and held back. We were both shaken by this paranormal occurrence. Words like unbelievable, unreal and incredible came tumbling out of our quivering mouths. It took a while for us to compose ourselves. The intriguing part was when Christi mentioned that she still struggled with Gertie's death and felt pushed to go to this event, but there were so many obstacles placed in her way, she wondered why she kept feeling hard-pressed to go. When Christi's eyes met mine, she automatically knew why. She made it a point to mention that next Sunday was Gertie's third-year death anniversary, which was just a week away. I was honored to be invited.

There probably were hundreds of churches among a million people in the San Jose area. Christi began attending this church not too long ago, which was a fair distance from where she lived. She could have chosen to sit in any of the dozens of empty seats and spaces, but right behind me was where she was probably led to sit. I could have also chose another topic to talk about but it was truly meant it all had to fit in perfect harmony.

I then went to another memory of Christi a few years later. I was in my car one morning listening to a spiritual program. I was so busy during that peak work time, that tuning into this station was a rarity. I began zooming in on the interview in progress and I was taken back as I was almost sure that it was Gertie's daughter, Christi, being interviewed. I waited with anticipation to hear her name. Minutes later, a confirmation—indeed it was Christi! It was again totally off the charts! It was probably a reminder that Gertie was right by my side.

I reached the driveway and went to bed contemplating true love and the amazing Gertie.

Enter and Win!

"The Red Gown" to be released soon. It is based on a true story and engages readers to question their beliefs about fate and destiny. This book is for readers who yearn for knowledge of the ethereal, insight into true love and life, and interested in reading the stunning journey of one woman.

Made in the USA
Monee, IL
05 July 2021

72945387R00020